Cricut Design Space

A Complete DIY guide To Learn How to Use the Best Tool to Start Cricut Projects

By Melissa Johnson

Table of Content

Introduction

Welcome to Cricut Design Space's comprehensive guide. Cricut is a device used for projects that are designed and cut. It offers you the ability to build various DIY designs, varying from cards the vinyl design invites and many more. No wonder what innovative concept you may have, with Cricut's help, you will possibly create it. Cricut has a free downloadable software named Cricut Design Space in order to be able to carry the designs out into the future.

Cricut Design Space is a Computer programming framework designed by the creators of the Cricut machine, Provocraft. Although the system itself makes the client, in a range of sizes, to cut numerous types and textual forms, the Cricut Design Space brings it to an undreamed level. Just attach the Cricut via a USB port to the PC, introduce the product, and unleash a completely different aspect of creativity.

The key benefit of the Cricut Design Space is the willingness of customers to weld or link letters together just to frame a solitary cut. The days of sticking each letter, in turn, are gone. Expressions of letters and shapes will currently be fastened together before cutting, making it easier and smoother to introduce cuttings to businesses than every time in modern memory. Another benefit of the Cricut Design Space is that before cutting, the shapes and letters may be managed extensively. Customers are only constrained to just adjusting the scale again, so now they will be willing to adjust the shape attributes to support their general design all the more probably. To get the exact look the crafter wants, each image may be stretched, rotated, and twisted. Although the Cricut Design Space has several advantages, the opportunity to merge pictures from multiple cartridges into one design is an undisputed top preference.

A perfect way to be a skilled crafter is to find a medium or partner that allows you the independence to pursue your passion. Cricut has created an awesome machine with advanced cutting technologies for anybody who wants to go into crafts, which can help you cut, design, and carry all your beautiful art ideas to life. To minimize your practice time and save yourself a lot of headaches, it is important to know what equipment and accessories to use for your Cricut! The Circuit machine is very flexible and can be used to assemble any project time that you can think of for many kinds of materials.

Apart from being a cutter of templates for a scrapbook, the Cricut machine has many purposes. Other items, such as wedding invitations, wall decorations, and so much more, can be created with the patterns themselves. You just have to think creatively. There are no barriers; even if there are any, they would only be a figment of your fantasy.

Chapter 1: All about Cricut

A Cricut is a cutter that helps you to cut and make stunning and gorgeous crafts from materials that you didn't realize existed. You can however draw, emboss and generate fold lines to make interactive creations, gift items, boxes, etc., based on the model you use. The Cricut cutting machine works, kind of, like a printer. You create a layout on your computer in the form of an illustration.

1.1 What is Cricut?

A Cricut is a specialized cutting device/machine that can be used to cut different materials for making crafts, projects, and much more. It cuts patterns, images, and text. Though many individuals contemplate a Cricut as the one that just cuts vinyl and card-stock, it may cut synthetic fabric, balsa wood, adhesive foil, and more. In addition to cutting, the machine has a writing and scoring connector with the Cricut machines: Explore One, Explore Air & Cricut Explore Air 2 (the latest versions offered by Cricut). A Cricut machine is common among craftsmen, party organizers, enthusiasts of DIY, and more.

The machines that have become accessible can also design with pens, compose with pens & score stuff for crisp, simple folding, in order to cut all kinds of materials.

What can a Cricut be used for?

Mentioning all will be a lengthy list- But, here's a quick list of things you can make with Cricut.

Projects for school- Cricut machines can be used for making school projects.

Card-stock projects- Designers & Event organizers can create greeting cards, event invites, and decorations for events, costume pieces, embellishments for Bible journals & much more.

Vinyl projects- For outside projects (possibly updating a mailbox) and kitchen products (such as cups) that might be washed by hands, use continuous vinyl. For fence patterns, make use of removable vinyl.

Iron-on patterns-Iron-on vinyl (often called heat transmission vinyl) is one of the most common uses for Cricut to produce personalized tops, bags, caps and much more.

Foam craft projects- For children's crafts, garlands, and more, craft foam projects are enjoyable.

Window grips projects– Think of making the window grips for vacations! With the Cricut machine, like the Preschool Design ideas, window sticking material is easily cut into various shapes and fixtures.

Cut & Print projects- The Cricut helps craftsperson to print pictures or images on their device and then cut with the Cricut in tandem with their home printer. There are several choices for personalized gifts or favoring for weddings, etc., from printer-friendly magnets to sticker paper.

Projects of faux leather - make elegant faux leather jewelry or fashion accouterments or apply a leather look to passes, cushions and more.

Projects of Adhesive Foil & Washi Sheet- For certain designs, adhesive foil & washi sheets are great. The adhesive foil brings a glossy, metallic appearance to every project.

Projects of stenciled wood - Use stencil vinyl to make your personal adhesive stencil, add it to wood & then dye. After the dye has settled, detach the stencil vinyl then there you go. Use stencil vinyl to make unique wood symbols and much more.

1.2 How Cricut Works?

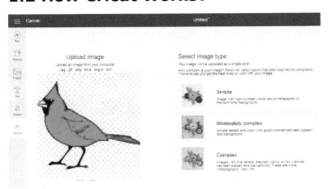

All of the Cricut machines are surely some of those machines that do amazing things. The cutting machine operates like a printer, kind of. You develop a layout in the form of a picture on your computer, then submit the image via a USB cable or a Bluetooth wireless link to the cutting machine.

There's a little computer in the machine which controls a cutting blade. It's almost about operating an inkjet printer using an ink nozzle. While the nozzle is instructed by a printer where to dump ink, the computer of the machine specifies the blade exactly when to make cuts.

The same way your cutting machine operates for writing, score, engraving, or embossing.

Your template will be sent to the cutting machine & the pen is instructed what to write by the computer inside. In order to create the invention, you designed, it can also command the numerous other tools to operate.

What is the Cricut machine equipped with?

There are numerous cutter types, and among them, the things that come with each machine varies. Yet, there are certain aspects that all machines come with.

Each package comes equipped with:

- The machine for cutting

- A fine-point quality blade and blade housing

- A mat for cutting

- A USB Cable

- A power connector

- A welcome guide for easy configuration

- Free trial membership for their software

- Access to at least 25 free projects that are ready-to-make

- Materials for a project to practice.

Many versions come with more items, such as various blades, scoring wheels, or a unique pen for writing.

1.3 Why Getting a Cricut?

There are thousands of examples for using a Cricut makes crafting life easier & better. Moreover, using a Cricut enables more design than anyone else had been doing, only because it's too simple to make stuff with a Cricut! None of this is to indicate that you can't make great projects by hand if you're not using a Cricut; a lot of things might be carved out of blades or perhaps an X-Acto knife. But using Cricut and WAY more efficiently is WAY easier than doing it by hand; still, Cricut will cut materials that are much tougher than one can do with scissors.

1. Incredibly flexible. More than 300 materials can be cut by A Cricut, and more can be scored, engraved, debossed, perforated, etc. A Cricut may create a different universe of opportunities that you can't do by hand, regardless of what type of crafting is involved, Do-It-Yourself (DIY) crafts, or interests you have.

2. It is reliable. A Cricut not only do lots of various tasks. However, it fixes them far more easily than you might ever do with the help of your hands. By effectively spacing the patterns it cuts on the material, it can preserve your energy, save you from tingling hands, and may also end up saving supplies and money.

3. it's smart to use. Although the machine could sound a little complicated at first, once you're comfortable with the fundamentals of the machine, it's quite simple to use.

4. To create cool things, you don't need to become a designer. While evaluating whether a Cricut becomes worthy for you, your specific design abilities are probably not a concern. You may create your own photos and graphics for your machine to use, but you can also produce hundreds of already designed pictures, graphics, & projects.

5. The Cricut devices are reliable and high-quality. The devices are well-built and made of quality components that do not ever tend to fray or split.

6. Cricut's machines are "long term." The Cricut Maker will use a lot of different blades and equipment for the latest Adaptive Tool System, and Cricut is still designing the latest tools for the maker. Each new kind of tool or blade brings a whole new range of outcomes for crafting, accessing the same device you have already! (Sadly, this latest equipment is not integrated with the Explore machines, but the Cricut Explore devices are also completely worth it because if you do not have to be trained to sculpt, deboss, perforate, etc. for the device, they will save you some money.)

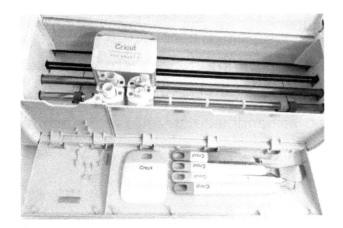

Who can use a Cricut?

Anybody can use a Cricut; it does not make a difference whether you are tech-savvy or not. The only thing that is really "necessary" to use a Cricut is wanting to manage things! If you think you're a craftsperson, DIY person, hobbyist, maker or some other kind of person who likes to create things with their own two hands, it's certainly worth buying a Cricut since you're going to have a lot of use out of it!

- **Cricut equipment is perfect for teachers;** you can use Cricut to make art sheets, school projects, holiday decorations, and loads of other fun things for your classroom.

- **For weddings, Cricut machines are excellent;** you can use them to create cake toppers, wedding invitations, name tags, and loads of other arrangements for the big day.

- **For owners of handmade stores,** Cricut machines are fantastic; you may use them on Etsy or that your own handmade store to manufacture or customize hundreds of online items you can offer.

- The Cricut machines are amazing for any form of the maker.

- If you are a crafter who has pain, muscle spasms, or some other kind of thing that affects your hands, a Cricut may be an amazing device.

Who cannot use a Cricut?

While nearly anyone can take benefit from using a Cricut, However, there are certain individuals that might not be worth a Cricut.

- If you like hand - made products, but you choose to purchase these on (ETSY) instead of creating them by your hands, a Cricut may not be for you. You're obviously not going to utilize a Cricut often to make it viable if you'd rather hire somebody else to create it rather than creating it yourself.

- While you love to do stuff, but you're super busy, and you're not really finishing the projects you're beginning, a Cricut might not be for you.

A Cricut may not be for you while you are an irregular crafter or enthusiast. It's actually not worth the expense if you just utilize the Cricut device either once or twice within a year. It's definitely not worth it, though you have an upcoming celebration or even you're a teacher. While you don't think you're going to use the Cricut device/machine either once or-twice a year.

Chapter 2: Cricut Model's Overview

Provo Craft and Novelty, Inc. developed the Cricut machines. The location of Provo Craft is in Utah. The business is fifteen years old yet was founded on December 21, 2003.

2.1 Old Cricut Machine Models

There were very solid old Cricut machines, plenty of buttons, recycled cartridges, and took very tiny cutting area- We should be glad that we have devices like Cricut Explore Air 2 and Maker today, but it might be a lot of fun to glance back at the past. Card makers and scrapbookers were genuinely targeted by inventive machines. Electronic cutting devices, at least within home craftsmen, were fairly novel and offered a better mode to do it all oneself from home. Currently, anything from creating vinyl decals & iron-on transfers to cloth & sewing designs and cutting cork or other forms of heat transfer is used by Cricut machines.

Following are the older Cricut machine models.

1. Original Cricut Machine

Although it might not be attractive, the device that initiated it all was the Cricut Personal. Cricut cartridges had been used by this device, and a computer wasn't required for it to operate.

It was a very trivial device/machine, with a rather tiny space for cutting. It was unable to render extremely complicated cuts, nor was it able to complete projects greater than 5.4 x 12 inches. The width of the cutting mat was just six inches broad, so it was just a simple handicraft machine used for cutting

2. Cricut Create

The next machine created by Cricut is the Cricut Create was (also normally recognized as Provo Craft back in the time). The Cricut Create machine was just a similar design as the 1st Cricut machine, although a few improvements were made. Compared to the 1st machine, it devises a completely new look and has the newest shades. It also enhanced the monitor panel. Technology and layout features were both expanded, and an eight-way rotating blade also came with it.

3. Cricut Expression

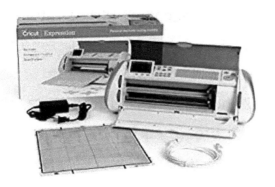

Next came the Cricut Expression, bringing some more substantive improvements. Most importantly, this was the 1st Cricut with a cutting capacity of 13 x 26 inches, and the minor cuts were better. A broader variety of materials could be sliced by Expression 1, including heavier products such as poster board & vellum.

It was still possible to use this machine individually without a machine, but the program for device use was certainly improving. Cricut Craft Room was the predecessor to Cricut Design Space, and the program was incomplete usage for the Expression.

4. Cricut Expression 2

A very famous machine in its time was the Cricut Expression 2. The machine's manner had changed; it came with a bigger, quicker, full-hued screen that made things much simpler. There were many wonderful features and enhancements to this machine, like:

- 1500+ designs already-loaded (text styles, pictures, quotes, etc.)

- Improved designs for manipulation-resizing, spinning, turning, mirroring.

- For more photos, use the Cricut Craft Room.

Cricut was progressively fetching more renowned and more famous among crafters by the time Expression 2 came out.

5. Cricut Imagine

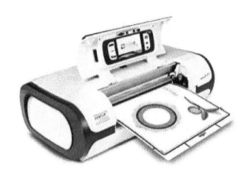

The Cricut Imagine machine is special since it is the sole machine that can print as well as cut. It was a printer & cutter by Cricut. In addition to the Imagine, to print and cut, you just ought to get a curvature cutting machine.

Ink for Cricut Imagine: Cricut partnered with HP to create a specially formulated black and three-colored ink to fit with the Envision. Unluckily, at the moment, the system was not the most successful for consumers, and it endured discontinued very soon, while Cricut tried developing machines that were more aligned with the real one.

6. Cricut Mini

The Cricut Mini cutting machine, you don't need to be mistaken with the Cricut Easy Press Mini, was just another little personal cutter. It was the 1st machine that required a computer to be used, with a narrower cutting range of 8.6 inches. While it wasn't as great a success as the Cricut Expression collection, this machine was marketed as a smoother, more portable, and simpler machine to move.

7. Cricut Cake

The Cricut Cake device remained part of the Martha Stewart Collection of Cricut Cake Machines. Actually, this device was used to decorate cakes, cookies and cupcakes. It could amend filo dough, sheets of frosting, gum paste, and much more.

2.2 Current Cricut Machine Models

With Cricut's brilliant collection of automated electronic cutting machines, all the anticipation, stress, and anxiety are stripped out of crafting, and you are ready to get creative and live the dream as the machine handles all the arduous bits for you. There are 3 Cricut devices for today's crafters to choose from. What is the Cricut Device, and what is the best one? In a nutshell, Cricut's devices are here.

The Cricut Maker, which deals with intense materials such as wood, leather & thinner metal and also more paper-friendly ones such as vinyl, cardstock and vellum, is the most flexible Cricut device, opening up a vast world of crating, with possibilities for draping and engraving, as well as cloth cutting. For craftsmen who prefer paper craft and card production, or vinyl-cutting designs, the Explore Air 2 machines are a strong match since they have the same roles as the Maker in these places, and both machines can accommodate cuts of up to 12 inches deep. The latest Cricut Joy is the beginner level crafting device, perfect for daily card making and label making, but this gorgeous Cricut machine has nothing ordinary! Its higher cutting width is 5.6 inches, but it can cut without a cutting mat, unlike the other two machines, utilizing a Smart Materials roll for long cuts of approximately 19 feet.

1. Cricut joy

The Cricut Joy is a tiny, lighter edition at 5'' x 8'' and less than 4 lbs. (introduced February 12, 2020-accessible March 2020). In the Cricut product line, The Joy adds two additional features not found elsewhere. The Joy is capable of cutting specific designs up to 4 feet long and frequent cuts up to 20 feet with advanced accessories and fabrics (labeled Smart Materialists).

Features

- Only Cricut device which can cut utilizing Smarter Materials without the need for a mat

- Tiny and portable for quick day-to-day crafts

- Using the complete Smart Materials roll, you can cut patterns approximately 21 feet lengthy.

- To cut amazing paper-cut cards for about 5.5 x7.25 in, use the inventive Enclosure Card mat with the already-scored card packs.

- Ideal for newbies to Cricut

Advantages

- The lowest cost rate of the three Cricut Smart Cutting Machines

- Best if you don't have ample space

- Easy and simple to configure

- Great for daily vinyl cards and labels

- Insertion of Card Mat & Card Packs ensures that a card that is bought from some shop would never be used again

Disadvantages

The minimum variety of products being cut by the least regulated machine.

- The pens for Cricut and equipment meant for the Maker and Explored Air 2 can't be used. Yet you have an additional Cricut device; you may require distinctive pens for Joy.

- The range of cut patterns is limited to 5.6" around.

- The mat which comes with the device only works on 4.3 x 6.6-inch products. There are wider mats that people might randomly purchase,

- The device only has a solo lock, so you can need to change tools if you'd like to both write and cut on the very same task.

What it'll cut?

Cricut Joy could cut about fifty materials, including acrylic, iron-on, cardstock, peel & gooey label paper, sticky foil, luxury paper, plastic chalkboard, sticker paper, sheet, iron-on, flat canvas, foil paper, shimmer cardstock, regular cardstock, swirl vinyl, Infusible Ink transmission papers, cardstock, acrylic, Smart Vinyl, Crafty Iron-On, window cling.

2. Cricut Maker

(Released August 20, 2017) With the Design Space, which is cloud-based, downloadable software, the Cricut Maker machine is used. It does not operate optimally. An internet link is needed when accessing Design Space on a desktop or laptop computer. You can use the offline functionality of that software by using the Design Space app on an iOS device (iPad/iPhone) to use your device and Design Space without an internet link. The Cricut Maker is a flexible machine with adjustable cutting and scoring heads.

Features

- The Maker is the device for you if you want the chance to develop the equipment and tools at your hands while your art skills grow.

- This is the Cricut series' most effective cutting machine; this can cut materials around 2.4 millimeters thick and gives up to 4 kg of power.

Advantages

- The Maker has all the functionality of Explore Air 2 and much more.

- The device comes with a revolving blade that enables the cutting of almost any material and the cutting of delicate papers like tissue paper.

- It has a comfortable pattern to stand up the tablet or phone while utilizing the Design Space software from one of these.

- Built-in storage gives you a convenient place to store tools and equipment in the body and parts of the device.

- When you have one, you would never wish to craft without it,

Disadvantages

- You would need to buy extra tools to maximize the usage of the Maker's more advanced features, such as engraving, rupturing, and forceful cutting.

- This is the maximum costly machine since it is the top-spec.

- It is the weightiest and biggest machine since it has to exert 4 k of cutting capacity.

- Without it, you will never wish to craft till you have one,

What it'll cut?

Cricut Maker will cut approximately 300 items, such as leather, acetate, plastic, balsa, bamboo linen, basswood, boucle, denim, broadcloth, burlap, calico, silk, cardstock, suede, Chantilly lace, sequins, duct tape tubes, copy paper, polystyrene foam, linen, art foam, crepe paper, tulle, double knit, pants, EVA foam, cotton, synthetic fur, synthetic brogues, felt, flannel, simple fabrics, etc.

3. Explore Air 2 by Cricut

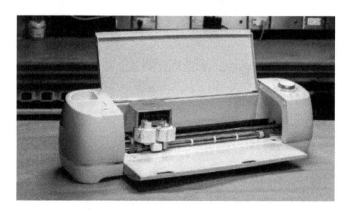

It cuts two times faster, a minor update from the Air. It comes in a number of shades and functions with the latest application for Circuit Design Space.

Features

- Quick Cut mode, which is ideal for designs that generate mass

- Cuts an extensive variety of products up to a thickness of 2mm

- The Shrewd Chooser material segment dial is simple to use and helps you to visually see if the machine is fixed to the right material

- You get a dazzling Yellow, Green Mint, or Multi Blue Cricut device with colorful models.

- Lightweight still fine design.

Advantages

- It will cut up to 11 x 22 inches of vinyl and decals that make it perfect for patterns that cover wide places, such as the facade of t-shirts and window glasses.

- For a short and simple finish, the machine can cut & score complicated present box layouts.

- There are two clamps in the machine. However, two separate tools may be used at a similar time.

- Incorporated storage offers you a convenient place to put tools and accessories in the frame and sections of the device.

Disadvantages

- There's a really loud Quick Cut feature. Use the normal cutting pace for a softer cut.

- It cannot cut very fragile items, such as tissue paper,

- A tool named scoring stylus must be purchased separately.

- Massive machine with a footprint that is just marginally minor than The Maker, but can cut with fewer materials

What it'll cut?

Around 100 products such as paper, acrylic, iron-on, cardstock, adhesive labels, foil, bamboo, canvas, sticker paper, art foam, cork, duct tape panels, thin synthetic leather, felt, plain cardboard, soft chipboard, shimmer paper, wax paper, washi paper, wrapping paper, plastic wrap, parchment, fused fabric & window cling can be cut by Cricut Explore Air 2.

4. Explore One by Cricut

Related to the other Explore machines, but with just a single holder for the tool. You can cut and compose, but in two steps, you have to do so.

Features

- Great starter machine at an incredible cost

- Cut, compose, and a score of 100 materials

- Sharp-Point Blade for a broad variety of common craft products for cutting

- Compatible with Deep-Point Blade, Scoring Stylus, and other tools (sold separately)

- Software Design Space® for iOS, Android, Windows®, and Mac®

- Free uploading of your own photos and fonts

- Compatible with cartridges by Cricut

What it'll cut?

Cricut Explore One is an easy-to-learn and simple-to-use digital cutting machine for DIY projects & crafts. One hundred materials, like cardstock, vinyl, and iron-on, to cut, compose, and score. This inexpensive machine makes it simple to fulfill your artistic idea, from cards to personalized T-shirts to home décor. The on-the-go interface on your laptop, smartphone, or iPhone. With thousands of pictures, fonts, and ready-to-make designs, browse and play. Or develop a layout of your own from scratch.

5. Cricut Explore

Each has a double tool holder for the Cricut Explore, Explore Air, and Explore Air 2 so that you can cut & write (or cut & score) in 1 phase. There is a single tool holder for the Explore One, so it can cut & write (or cut & score) in 2 stages.

Explore Air & Explore Air 2 have built-in Bluetooth, so you would need a Cricut Wireless Bluetooth Adapter to use it with your mobile iOS or Android smartphone or to cut wirelessly from your phone to Explore One and Explore

6. Cricut Air Explore

This is a wireless gadget that can cut paper and more into cloth. It works with the existing application of Circuit Design Space.

Chapter 3: Cricut Design Space

Cricut Design Space is the design app from Cricut that helps you to cut with the Cricut Maker & Cricut Explore machines. The oldest software classified as Cricut Craft Room has been used by older machines such as Cricut Expression 2 and Cricut Mini. Design Space is a Mac or PC device downloadable app that helps you to make original designs and import ready - made designs, or to use them free of charge or to buy designs specifically into Design Space. Even on your Android or iOS smartphone you can use the Design Space Software, although it does have more functionality limitations. If you do have an older machine cartridge, you may connect it to your Design Space account and then use the cartridge with your newer Cricut machine. The Cricut Explore has a slot for cartridges so you can bind your cartridges a bit more conveniently. After you have connected your cartridges to any device registered with you, you might use your design in Design Space

3.1 What is Cricut Design Space?

Design Space is software from Cricut that can be downloaded to your Windows computer for free. On the program, you will find prepared layouts which you can cut with the machine immediately, or you can upload pictures, fonts (or including your own!) of Cricut to create something more unique. Around 75,000 pictures, 400 fonts, and more than 800 predesigned Make it now designs are lodged in Cricut Design Space. The projects for Make It Now is already completed for you, and all you have to do is click on "Go."

How can you get Design space?

In order to download the software to your computer, go to design.cricut.com. You can make an account after its downloaded and start using it instantly.

Is Cricut Design Space free of cost?

You can download the software for free, and you can discover some available Cricut fonts & photos to use right away. In the Design Space, you can even use your own device's fonts and upload image files into the program to be used. You may pay a small charge to use specific Cricut images & fonts or pay a recurring fee for Cricut Use, which requires you to use Design Space's wide catalog of images and fonts.

There are several characteristics; it's challenging to know where to begin.

Home Screen

When you start the Cricut Design Space, it's the first window you can see.

On the top left (that's the menu), you'll see 3 rows accompanying "Home," then "Welcome, then "My Projects.

Afterward, you can pick the Cricut Machine Form from the drop-down board (whether in Cricut Maker/Cricut Explore Family), then finally the icon "New Project."

Cricut advertisements are preceded by (at the top of the main screen) My Projects (projects that are all retained), Cricut Access (ventures that you may purchase a paid plan or use with the Cricut Access affiliation), professionally prepared Projects (projects produced by talented designers), most famous Video Seminars, and finally some rows of ideas for seasonal projects. Let's have a view of the topmost left corner of the "Three Lines" menu bar.

Open/View Profile

You may update the line "About Me," profile image and access you're publicly available projects here. All of these are elective and not necessary to practice Cricut Design Space (however useful if you choose to make shared projects with someone else)

Home Screen

It takes you directly to the key screen.

The Canvas

Take you to the canvas, the core portion of the design space that you're going to use.

A little farther down, you'll see all the info on your canvas.

New Machine Configuration

If you have a brand new, unopened Cricut Maker, Cricut Explore, or Cricut Easy Press 2 machine, this is the point to set it up, configure, or upgrade it.

Calibrating

Calibration choices for the Revolving Blade, fine Blade (knife), & Printing Then Cut can be found here.

Managing Specific Materials

Here you can notice all the substantial adjustments you have attached to the machine.

The Term, Cut Weight, Several-Cut, and Blade Style settings may be adjusted for every sort of material.

You may even select a new material if you're clicking the whole ways to the end of the screen.

Firmware Upgrade

That really seems to be where you actually go to modify the wired machine firmware you've got.

It's a brilliant idea to monitor this timely.

Details of accounts

You can access information about your accounts here, such as account settings, payment configurations & affiliation data.

Connection of Cartridges

You will connect up these here while having some Cricut cartridges. This can be done only on a laptop, MacBook or desktop.

Cricut Access

You may log in to Cricut Access and track your subscription here. It's much better than purchasing particular items, plus there are too many pictures, fonts, and designs from which to choose.

Setups

You may adjust the settings of the grid of Design Space here and move the measuring units between Metric and Imperial.

Legal

You would press here to give a read to the entire Cricut machine the "fine print."

Latest functionalities

Here more details on new features can be found.

Country

You may change the country here. Australia, the UK, as well as the US are among the choices.

About Help

This leads you to Support Hub, where FAQs, tips, repair, fix, and more can be found.

Signing Out

You will log out of your account of Design Space here.

Reviews

Clicking here opens up a page where suggestions and comments may be left. Now that Home Screen, as well as the menu at left, has been protected, it is ready to be in the mince and bones of the Design Space: Canvas.

The Canvas

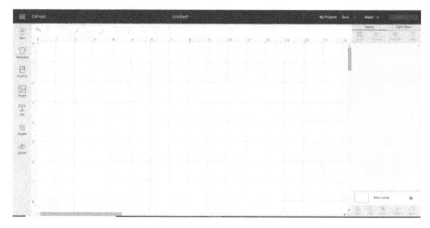

That's the workshop for your Cricut for creating things. You'll see this screen the most. It includes a wide glided work zone with top functions, a left-hand menu, and the right-hand Layers & Pigment Sync Palettes.

Let's look in-depth at each portion.

Canvas: Menu on the Left

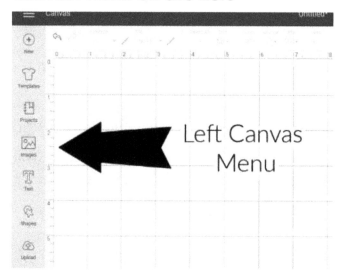

Left Canvas Menu

New

To begin with, a new canvas, click New. Make sure to backup it before you make a fresh canvas if you're doing work on a layout that you need to hold. If you like to conserve, Design Space may query you until it dissipates it off.

Patterns/Templates

There are predesigned models that can be used with your project to ensure that the projects are the required size. Tons are available to pick from.

You will choose various choices after you have selected a design. Also, you can change the template hue to anything you want.

Adjust template color

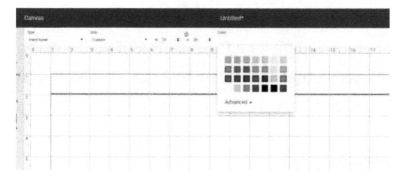

Click the prototype stratum at the end of the palette of layers to remove the template, and then click the erase icon.

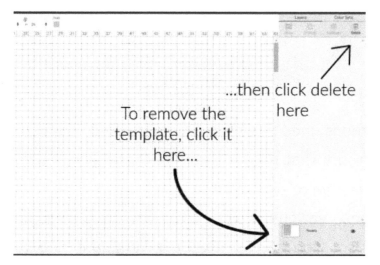

...then click delete here

To remove the template, click it here...

In the design space, delete a prototype. The low-profile, lightweight Bright Pad makes it easy to craft while lowering eye pressure.

The Projects

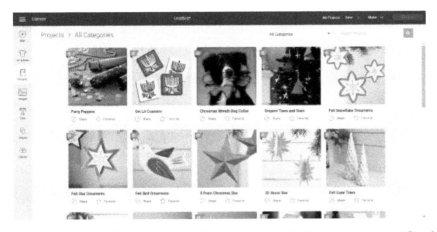

Here each of the already prepared designs specified in the Design Space and those you have uploaded can be found.

Drop-down Projects menu of Design Space

Pictures

You'll notice all the photos accessible in Design place under Photographs (and there's a Ton of them).

A number of the photos are provided with an Access membership of Circuit. "On the upper left, they have a green button, "a." And also, for those that are free for all, there is a handful that you do need to order.

You can select Categories appearing on top, and it takes you to the Featured Categories screen ("Free the Week" right now, "Most Common," and "Newly Added"). In Design Space, picture categories, you'll see common types like "Birthday," Anniversary," as well as "fall" below that. You'll discover categories with labels like Martha Stewart, Disney and Marvel if you scroll down beyond that.

If you're pressing 'Filter' on the top right of the search bar, you may filter photos by property (My images, posted, free, Cricut Entry, and purchased), form (3D objects, context & borders, textures, envelopes and cards, photos, sentences, and printable), as well as layers (multi-layer, single layer).

Cartridges are next to the Groups. You will find collections of pictures there, all of which go together.

The Design Space menu for cartridges

To connect it to the canvas, just press the picture and then clunk Attach Photos. Next to the cartridges, there is even a explore bar. Type in something you're searching for, and you're going to catch some fantastic choices to apply to your theme.

Text

Text Tool

To apply the text to the canvas, click here. You may use a range of fonts that you can buy (most of which are included along with access to Cricut) and use fonts that you have imported on the desktop.

Shapes

You can place simple shapes like rectangles, circles, squares, polygons, stars etc., on the canvas here. It's also where you might find score marks, which you can position with a Scoring stylus or scoring wheels on your photos to use. If there are some pieces to fold in your idea, that's where you'd like to position a score mark.

Uploading

This is where you do it if you devour any SVG and PNG image file to add to your project. Click Insert Picture and scan your device for a photo, and then click the Upload icon. Name the picture format, apply tags, and press the save icon.

Image Name and Tag - Design Space

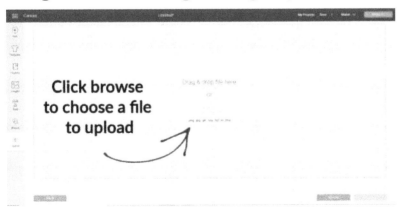

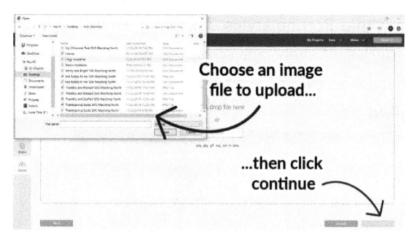

Choose an image file to upload...

...then click continue

Pick the imported file to attach the picture to the canvas and select Upload Photos.

Give your image a name and some tags so it's easy to search for, then click Save

A Design Fill may also be uploaded on the uploading screen. Select Upload Template and select your .jpg, .gif, or .bmp file pattern or picture.

Now, let's have a peek at the menu for the central canvas.

Key Menu for Canvas (Across Top)

Top Menu of Canvas

There are some items in the central menu crosswise the topmost of the canvas that you can use often.

Now one by one, let's have a peek at them.

Line-typing

With numerous fine point blades, guides, and pens, the Line-type drop-down menu has many choices to use.

Cut, Break

The Good Point, Intense Cut, Knife (Cricut machine - Maker), Gyratory (Cricut Maker), & Fused Cloth blades are used to cut fabrics.

Draw

With each of the Cricut pens, draw on the materials.

Scoring

Using single or even duple scoring wheels (Cricut Maker) or Stylus for scoring to score materials.

Engraving

The Inscription Tip engraves materials. (Only at Cricut Maker)

Deboss

Deboss the supplies/materials with Debossing Tip. (Only at Cricut Maker)

Wave

Using the curly edge blade to carve a curly edge pattern onto fabrics. (Only at Cricut Maker)

Perf

The Perforation Blade enables perforated surfaces to be quickly broken off. (Only at Cricut Maker)

Material Menu Color

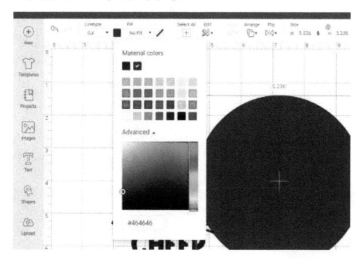

Here, you may adjust the picture layer's hue to fit the material you are going to use.

Zero or no Fill

Pick zero-fill while you just want the supplies being cut, and with Print Then Cut, no fill hue shades, or design would be added. To cut layers, that's the default mode.

Printing

If you select to use the Print, Then Cut feature, pick it. Below, you'll see the two choices.

Color

Before cutting, choose the color you would like to copy on the photo.

Design

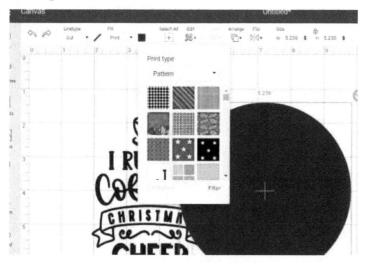

Until cutting, pick a design you'd want to facsimile on the picture. After selecting a template, in the lower-left portion of the main toolbar, you can tap Edit Pattern to amend the dimension and position.

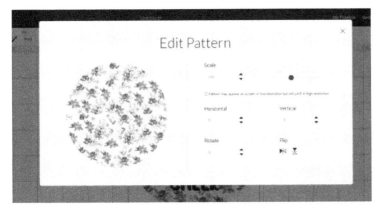

Edit Screen Pattern Space Design

Choose All

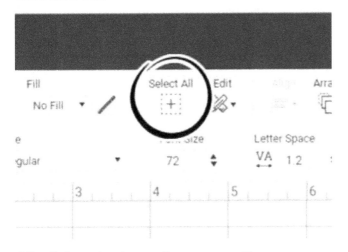

All of the stratums/layers on the canvas are picked. Click on the button once more to unselect anything if you gobble chosen something.

Editing

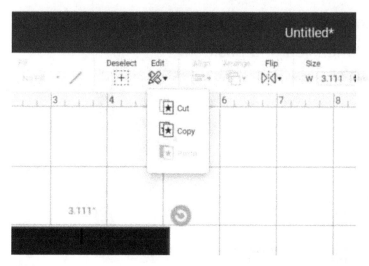

Cut: Cut a photo from canvas

Copy: On a canvas, copy a picture

Paste: Paste on canvas the cut or derivative picture

Set or Align

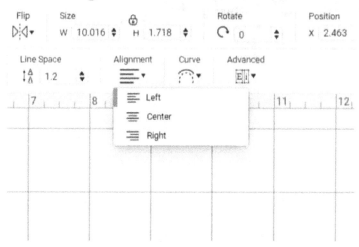

You may press this to dispose of them in various ways when you have two or even more icons selected. If you have several images picked, this menu often helps you to divide these vertically or horizontally.

Arranging

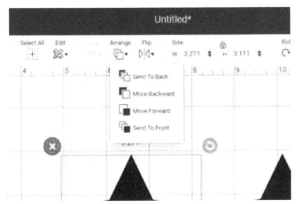

Shift to back: Shift to the rear, the selected picture.

Move Backward: Move one layer back, the selected picture.

Move Forward: Move one layer forward, the selected image.

Shift to Front: Move towards the front, the certain image you have selected.

Flip

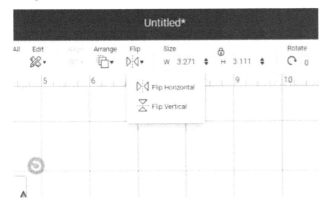

Horizontal Flip: Flip a picture from left towards right.

Vertical Flip: Flip the picture from the top pointing towards the end.

Magnitude

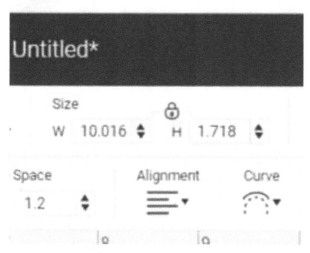

W (Width): Configure the size of the picture

H (Height): Configure the altitude of the image.

Choose the lock symbol to change the display size of the file (like whether you want to adjust the height, or conversely, but maintain the diameter the same).

Rotating

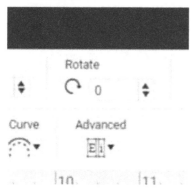

Rotate your picture to whatever range of degrees you like.

Spot/position

X-axis: Parallel spot

Y-axis: perpendicular spot

You likely won't use this function regularly, but for whatever reason, if you import a picture and it's off-screen, you can adjust the X & Y to nil so that you don't have to scroll to plaid it.

Writing/Texting Menu

The textual menu remains underneath the menu bar at the uppermost corner.

The fonts

Tap the Downward Arrow button here, and the font styles menu will appear.

It is necessary to classify "All" (Machine & Cricut fonts), "System" (System fonts of the laptop), and "Cricut" (Paid & free fonts are accessible on Design Space by Cricut. Most of them would be included with your membership if you do have Cricut Access.)

Searching Bar

You can enter the font here and check by name if you know all the details of the font style that you are searching for.

Filter

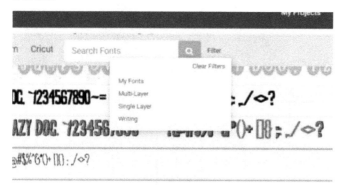

You will filter The Fonts (this includes your computer fonts and your account fonts if you are a user of Cricut Access), Multi-Layer (fonts with far more than one layer to be ripped), Sole Layer (fonts with one layer to be ripped) also Writing (fonts with one sheet to be cut) (fonts that are a single line and will work with Cricut Pens or the Engraving or Debossing tool).

Styles

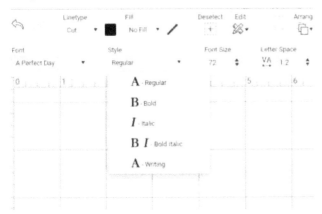

To pick a text grace, press the Downward Arrow here. You may see only a couple of these choices, based on the font you have chosen.

Regular: The default edition

Bold: Thick style

Italic: Distorted edition

Bold Italic: Sturdier and skewed version

Writing: Edition of Single Line (impeccable for Pens used by the Cricut, Etching Tip & Debossing Trick)

Reading Italic: The skewed edition of a single line (also perfect for Cricut Pens, Engraving Trick, and Debossing Trick)

Size of Font

Make the text greater or minor.

Another alternative: The size of the box can also be adjusted by pressing and moving a dual blue arrow in the lower right-hand corner.

Letter Space

Adjust the level of space that the letters have between them.

Another alternative: you may also activate the letters & push these where you like them if you can't quite get it correctly.

Line Space

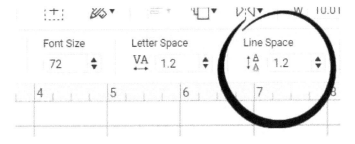

The sum of space among the lines of the text can be changed here.

Other alternatives: You can even activate text lines if you can't get it exactly perfect, then you can push them wherever you want.

Alignments

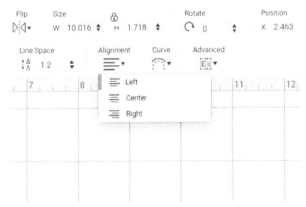

To adjust the text orientation to Left, Middle, or Right Centered, press the Downward Arrow here.

Curve

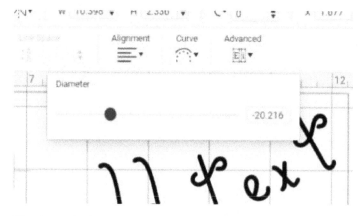

To bend the text in round or up, use this method. Move the knob to the left: The text's margins are formed upwards.

Move the knob towards the right side: the edges of the written material would be curved downwards. Even in the box, you can insert a particular number. Negative values position the edges upwards, and the edges downwards are angled by positive numbers.

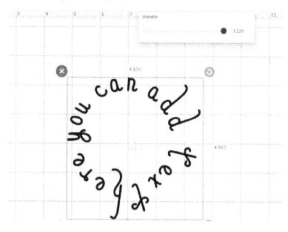

Note: The written material can be shaped into a circle if you move the knob the whole way to the left or right margin.

Design Space Curve Tool

Advanced ones

	Rotate		Position			
H 2.354 ↕	↻ 0 ↕		X 1.908 ↕	Y 1.986 ↕		

ignment   Advanced

≡ ▾   ▣ ▾

9	10	▣ Ungroup To Letters	13	14
		▣ Ungroup To Lines		
		▣ Ungroup To Layers		

For various text ungrouping choices, press the Down Arrow button that you may utilize to adjust the placement of the text and categorically modify the appearance.

Deselect words

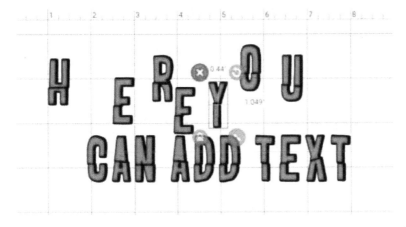

This released the characters so you may independently move them.

For template fonts, this choice is a necessity. Mostly with Letter Space adjuster, you can somewhat adjust the space, but to catch the slashes/lines to link, it typically also takes some tweaking.

Ungroup Lines

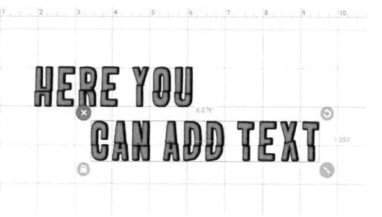

This released text lines but leaves the letters clustered together in - line such that the gap between texts lines can be changed however you wish.

Ungrouping the layers

HERE YOU
HERE YOU
CAN ADD TEXT

Whether you have chosen a miscellaneous font, it releases the layers/sheets; thus, they could be individually transferred, changed, or removed.

Zoom In & Out

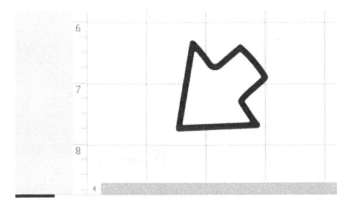

There are minus and plus buttons on the lower-left crook of the panel canvas that you might custom to zoom in and out of the project.

LAYERS

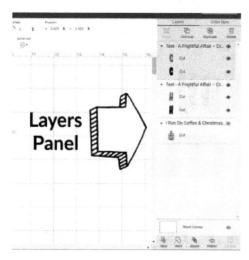

Layers
Panel

You can see the stratums of the project here. Each element of the project has a layer of its own. You can control each sheet in numerous ways by using the Layers/Sheets menu.

Let's have a little better expression at each method from the Layers Panel.

Menu with Top Layers

Group

Using this method to link your project photos, text, & layers around so you may shift or scale them quickly. In

Design Space, they only stay clustered on canvas, and once you submit these to be trimmed, they can detach on the required color-based mat.

Ungroup

Using it to ungroup whatever is clustered together.

Duplicates

To create a replica of a certain layer, press this icon.

Delete

To erase the chosen layer, press here.

Menu for Bottom Layers

Cut

Slicing two overlapping forms into different pieces. You can cut a form obtainable of the other shape and use this by sawing parts off with the other shape to crop shapes. This option is only possible if you've picked two layers.

Weld

Merge three or more shapes that intersect or move structured into one narrative format. In edict to construct a consistent outline with Weld, it is necessary to touch the pieces.

There's not an UnWeld button at this point. Clicking on "Undo" might be the only option to unwind shapes.

While you weld a chunk of the project, thus start working on it and reminisce that you want to unweld; after soldering, you will have to remove all the work you did.

Weld is a quite useful tool, and you're likely to practice it a bunch; just ensure that while you do this, you're able to constrain

Connect/Attach

The Attach tool joins three or more stuff together or maintains them on the Cricut mat used for cutting in the same specific position. For starters, you can apply the written sheet/layer onto the picture you would like to have some written material on it in the design by using Cricut pens. Also, if there are score lines for your project, you would like to connect these to the side of the venture that you need to score.

Unlike the group, connect retains the parts and also the canvas on the Cricut mat (used for cutting) around. You may go posterior and even remove the bits if you need to, something you can't do for Weld.

Flatten

This tool connects together or holds two or more items in the same REL Flatten for printing and cutting; this attribute can be used. This transforms every photo into a file that can be accessed. If you're attempting to print a layered template, flatten it first, combining several layers into a single sheet that can be printed on the printer and afterward cut with Cricut. There is no unflatten key; however, if you want to go back, you'll have to press 'Delete' to change and redo the colors or theme.

The Contour

You may "switch on" or "switch off" portions of a picture using this tool. Pick the file, press Contour, & a window opens up whither you may individually select each section of the picture to erase it. You could go away and bring these back on if you change your opinion. This allows it to delete a portion of a pattern you don't want. Contour can work only if ungrouped is the picture you chose. If the picture would be welded or cut after that, you're not going to allow to switch the initial pieces back off or on, only an FYI.

Sync of Color

You will match the layers' colors here so that you use fewer materials.

If you have double purple layers as well as an orange layer, for example, and you want to shift one of the purple sheets to orange, you could go to the Color Synchronization menu and simply move it downwards to the layer you prefer.

Mat Preview Screen "Make It"

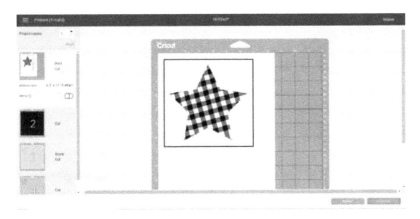

Copies of Project

Without needing to switch to the canvas, apply more versions of your designs to your mats. Adjust the amount to the desired quantity and press Apply.

Mats

There could be one or more mats to remove, based on how many colors the project has. They are listed in the direction in which they go, and next to them, it tells whether the photo is going to be drawn, cut, and scored, respectively.

Size of Material

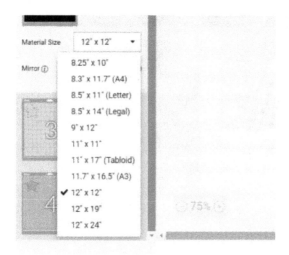

You may adjust the size of the material for the mat here. To pick from, there are many choices. Also, you can adjust the size settings here if you have an 11-22 inch mat. Design Space may ask you whether you are using an 11 x 22-inch mat or whether you want to move back and adjust your image if your picture reaches the 11 x 11-inch mat dimension.

Here, you can also transfer the pictures around on the mat. Just press the photo and slog it onto your mat where you want it to be. Until you cut it, make sure you have the material positioned at the correct point on the mat.

Menu of Three Dots

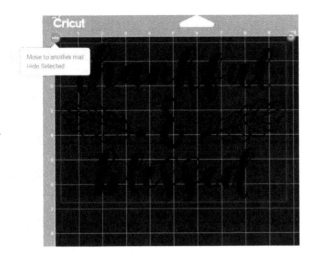

You could even select Move to some other mat or Hide Selected if you click on the three dots in the upper left corner of the image on the mat.

You may select Switch to some other mat or Hide Specified if you press the three dots in the upper left corner of the picture on the mat.

Switch to a new mat

This transfers the photo to one of the mats & changes the similar shade.

Hide selected choices

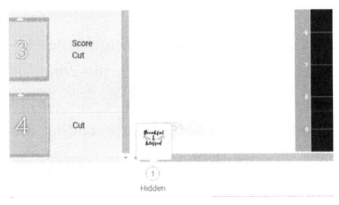

This will mask the photo from the mat so that it will not be cut. At the end of the page, an icon appears that you can press to mask the image.

Summary

You may practice all you have learned here and use it in numerous ways with your incredible Cricut machine to create some seriously cool stuff.

3.2 How to Upload Pdf Sewing Patterns In The Cricut Design Space?

The 1st thing to keep in mind is that a PDF template cannot be exported directly to the Design Space, so you need to transform the pattern into a compatible image-type format. Don't worry; it's simple to do this.

First of all, open the PDF file in the Acrobat Reader that you want to import. In the upper toolbar, click the 'More Tools' icon and then choose' Fit on One Whole Page'-this adjusts the picture to fit the screen and render it ready for conversion.

Then select and 'zip' the screen area covering the pattern piece as well as its square test/sizing. Click the Windows symbol plus Shift Key plus S concurrently to pull up the template snip feature and, using your cursor, cut out the design piece image along with the test/size square box and SAVE IT as a .jpg or .png file with your now complete page pattern image on the screen before you. (As an aside, you can always print your design out and follow the directions for downloading the paper patters below if you find this section a little confusing

Do this for all relevant pieces, ensure that every piece has a size test square next to it since this is important to accurately size the pattern piece until it has been uploaded in Design Space. Activate Cricut Design Space now and pick a 'New Project' to open the blank canvas screen.

From the project toolbar, press 'Upload.'

To view your freshly saved .jpg or .png pattern images, click on 'Upload Picture' and then 'Browse.' If the file has been recovered by Design Space, save it as a 'Complex' image, as this helps you to wipe up and delete any places you don't need, as well as maintain the lines sharp.

Using the 'Select & Erase' feature, you need to remove all places that are not a member of the pattern piece; then, your final picture is only the pattern section and the size square.

Click 'Continue'. The option to save the file as a 'print then cut file' or as a basic 'cut image' is then given to you. In particular, the arrow that tells the position in which the template should be cut from the fabric (e.g., considering the direction of your fabric's grain or greatest stretch).

Upload it into the blank project canvas until saved.

As you'll see, the upload pattern piece is a bit small-sized to the dimension of the Design Space canvas; here's where the sizing box steps in.

So, you have to adjust the file now. The most precise approach to do this is to build a square (using the shapes box in the leftmost toolbar) of the same size/scale as the measuring box of the pattern parts, e.g., it should be 1.5" here. Now resize your pattern picture (by clicking on the pattern piece and choosing the resizing tab at the bottom right) and drag before the sizing box 'grows' enough to precisely and effectively overlay the square, like this... (Remember that at this point, your sizing box & your pattern piece are related, because if you increase the size of one, you're raising the size of the other automatically.

If you intend to make sure that you have them the exact same size, Zoom in then.

Tada! Now your pattern piece must be measured properly. Next, we just need to move it so that the grain-line of the pattern parts is moving in the right course.

There are only a couple of basic steps left to take first. Otherwise, your Cricut would try to take those out of your expensive fabric, too; it is better to get rid of such test/sizing squares! At this point, the sizing box & your pattern piece are still connected as one image; you need to separate them now. Upturn the size of the red box first and use it to fully overlay the size box to 'strip' it out (using the 'Slice' feature) before removing all of them.

Now that your template pieces are a) correctly shaped, b) positioned in the correct direction, and c) the measuring boxes have been eliminated, we need to turn the pattern piece into some kind of basic cut file (Know that it originally held as a Print & Cut file to see the grain-line key)

Looking at the 1st chosen picture, you will find that the type of line is 'Cut', and 'Print' is the fill image. Select the Fill alternative and adjust it to 'No Fill'; this transforms the pattern piece to a basic cut file automatically; if handled properly, it will 'grey out.'

Finally, one really the last thing! Adjust all the template parts you cut out of the same cloth to one tone.

AND you are done. Select 'Make It' now and get the Cricut to cut your pattern out for you.

3.3 How to Upload A Paper Sewing Pattern To Design Space?

The method of importing a paper pattern is almost precisely the same as uploading your transformed PDF pattern files; you only need to bring the paper pattern files first onto your computer-for this, you would need access to a scanner if you don't have one installed, visit your local library as they are probably to have one.

Cut out the bits of paper template, parting an mm or 2 of paper along the pattern line as they have to be clearly visible to work correctly with this! Then cut out in the same fashion across the test square.

Place the pattern piece on the skimming plate, face down, and place your square size box next to it and scan it into the system (preferably one pattern piece at a time). Scan in and proceed ahead.

To save your .jpg file, press 'Save As,' rename your file, and select the ultimate folder.

Now you can continue uploading to Cricut Design Space from the 5th step in the above PDF tutorial.

The 'Images' tab,' Shapes, & 'Upload' are the three separate positions you can add designs on your mat. Images are the place where you can find everything the Cricut offers. Free pictures are accessible, and premium images are accessible and are included in Cricut Access (a subscription service). For specific photos of festive holidays (like the train for this party). Shapes are convenient, so you don't have to select a lot. There will be two separate options when you select 'Upload.' There's [a cut image] and Template Fill to upload.

IMPORT SVG PICTURES TO DESIGN SPACE

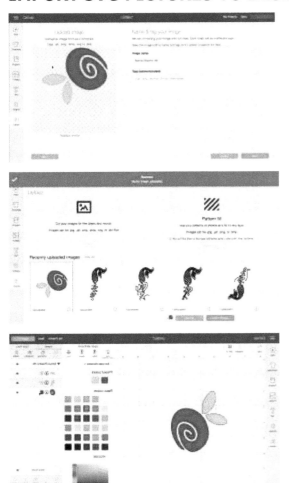

The simplest form of an image to upload in Design Space is SVG Photos. This is usually what you might buy if you accessed a 'Cut' file (like our Fresh Cut SVG Bundles). SVG refers to Versatile Vector Graphic, and that ensures that without compromising quality, you can size it up or down. Within the Design Space App, these photos still have the most modification choices, and that is because it integrates each cut as a separate item. Bear in mind that it would appear even more daunting in the layers tab if you upload a larger file because there is a layer created for each cut.

To upload every file type, use the up arrow to enter the little cloud icon. Click the [cut file] upload button and pick your file. This will open up the display where you might name and apply keywords to your file. Then you should click Insert Picture, and your canvas would be placed into it. It would look like one piece when you tap on the layout and move it around. After all, everything holds together. But note that each piece is a separate layer now in the layers tab on the right? You may change each piece's color and break it off with contrasting maps. Hit MAKE IT (top right) when you've adjusted it to your liking and see how the items spread out on the mat.

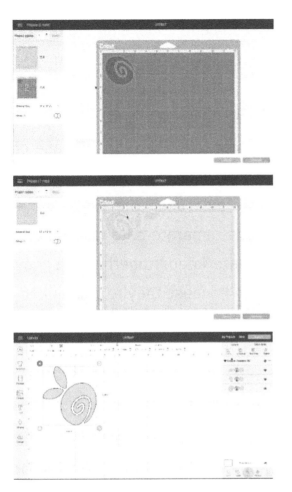

They're on mats individually. They are, of course, since they are of distinct colors because you need two contrasting vinyl colors. You'll actually go back to render all the pieces one hue and try again if you're anything like me. But the style is all muddled, you'll find. Here's the reason. By organizing all the various parts for you on your mat, Cricut Design Space aims to allow the most use of every other bit of vinyl. This could save vinyl, but if you tried to keep it lined up by hand, it could be a pain in hand. Go back to the canvas and choose all the design pieces. By bringing down (Control, CTRL) on the keyboard and clicking all the layers on the layer screen, you can do this, or you can just click and move your cursor over the layout to select all. Then, at the base of the layer board, press the little Attach (paper clip) button (highlighted in blue). This would keep the whole piece intact without destroying the separate data completely. You can see that the template keeps together this way when you click 'make it.' And because they're only linked, you can split them and adjust the size of one piece at any time or opt to remove the purple rose and the green leaves.

IMPORT PNG Photos TO DESIGN SPACE

With Cricut, PNG files are the most used ones. PNG refers to Portable Network Graphic, a lossless file format for image segmentation. It implies that it has a lot more details than a JPG (for instance), and the *biggest* part is that it can provide a clear context that makes it very easy to import and use for cutting. This is the sort of file used for Cricut MOST frequently. The images are uploaded as ONE layer, ensuring they can stay together and cut just as they are imported. What is that supposed to mean? When imported, you cannot conveniently adjust the color of one section of the design or reorganize the letters of a design.

You tap the little 'Upload' with the cloud again to upload a PNG with a translucent background, and you'll have a couple more measures than you did with the PNG. You will be asked to choose if it is a simple, moderately complicated, or complex picture after selecting your file. Then you'll be taken to a page where any sections you don't like can be erased. You should skip over this stage for a file that already has a translucent background & no pieces you don't really like. You would then be asked to select either print and cut for your Upload or just an image cut only. Choose to cut only, and your template will be loaded into the picture gallery you have submitted and can be inserted on your canvas.

You will see that it has a translucent backdrop until it's on the canvas; you can switch it around and resize it much like the SVG, except you'll find in the layer panel there's only one layer. This ensures that you can't just pick the light-bulb and print it on a new mat in a different color (although you might repeat it and draw the lines to distinguish the pieces. You'll find it when you press 'Make It' because it's all on one layer, the bits don't bounce around. It will cut everything in the same layout in which you uploaded it, making it simple to add the transfer tape and pop it on your surface.

IMPORT JPG Photos TO DESIGN SPACE

JPG is a type of photographic file named after the group named the file type. It's great for pictures as it effortlessly treats all the colors, but it can't have a translucent background. This implies that while you are importing the picture into the Design Space software, you need to adjust.

You'll note that it's not all black and transparent (because it's a JPG); it has some brightness. To make it easier to remove. This is what you're going to want to do to make things easy to get a quick range for a photo to print and then cut. If you run in Procreate, you can even do a PNG with the white background and send it without the grey background. But it's the very same moves as you try to upload it in. You may need to do a little more in this tab, depending on your picture, before going on. You can select either print then cut or a cut only picture when you move to the next page. You will see how smooth the cut lines are on the picture only cut-how that's you realize in the previous tab you don't have much special to delete.

So, in your uploaded pictures, it will populate, and you may insert it on your canvas.

Like a PNG, you'll note that there's just one layer in the layers tab. Instead of the layer-cut symbol, you can see a printer instead. It will load into its own print when you press 'Make it' then cut mat (mat with a black sensor box around it). You'd print it from here and then cut it.

HOW TO USE JPG PHOTOS FOR FILL PATTERNS (TWO WAYS)?

You'd take precisely the same measures as the above JPG picture (without erasing the background). When you embed it, apply the shape that you want the pattern to fill in. Exactly where you want the pattern to fill, place your shape over your design. When you are done, you can resize the pattern and switch it around as well. Then, by retaining CTRL on the keyboard and clicking all layers on the layer panel, click all layers OR you can either press and drag your cursor over the template and shape to choose both of them. Then, at the bottom of the layer page, click 'Slice.' This will provide you with three layers. In addition to the layers you don't want to use (or just remove them), you can press the little eye so that you are left with your pattern-filled form.

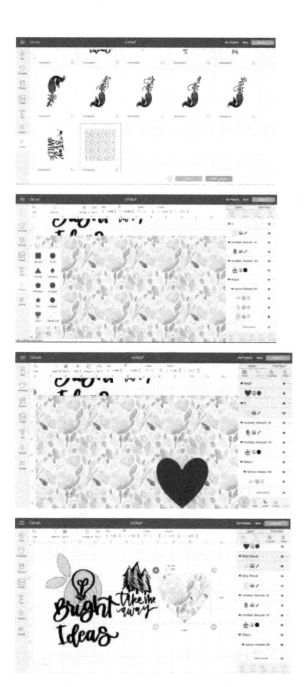

Uploading your watercolor floral (design) as a Pattern Fill rather than under the default Upload is the other option you can get this effect. You have two options when you go to the upload tab (that little cloud). You choose your pattern, and then, before you save it, you can have to name or title your pattern. When you go back to your gallery of posted pictures, you'll notice that it isn't there. That's because the patterns have been preserved, not the pictures. In the layers tab, you need to pick the shape or picture that you want to fill with the pattern first and then transform it into a print (not just a cut). Then, in the layers tab, you can see the 'Patterns' choice, and the pattern will pop up there. It will be applied to your shape when you pick it.

3.4 What is Access by Cricut?

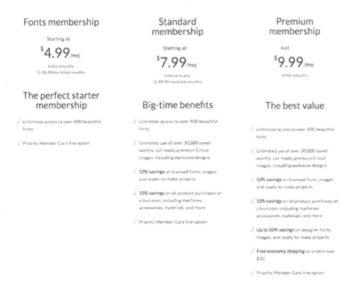

Cricut Access is a Massive library that will help you choose and create designs that have already been designed. If you're just getting started, this is really useful. You can have exclusive fonts, icons, 3D projects if you have Cricut Access, and depending on the project you have, and if you can think about anything, you have it. For any occasion and any products, you want to work with, they have been designed. This is pretty impressive. Cricut Access is a premium subscription that allows you immediate access to an enormous archive of over 90,000 images, millions of fonts, and projects ready to be cut. You can get other perks, such as discounts on approved images, fonts, and interactive items, based on the package you have.

Font Subscription

The Cricut Access - Fonts subscription is the first one. Cricut contains over 400 fonts, and whether paid yearly (in a lump sum) or $6.99 a month if billed,

This subscription costs as little as $4.99 a month.

Standard Subscription

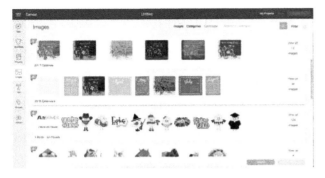

The Cricut Access - Standard is the next tier. You can browse 400+ fonts and also 30,000+ images and cut files with this subscription. In addition, this package gives a 10 percent discount, with certain exclusions, on pictures and fonts not included in the subscription, and also on product purchases.

It is also mandatory to pay this subscription monthly or yearly. Normal memberships commence yearly at $7.99 a month or weekly at $9.99 per month. On this package, yearly subscribers save $24.

Premium Subscription

The Cricut Access - Premium is the final tier (and best overall value). The Premium membership is just that,

Premium! It covers all fonts, all photos but still has a half-off discount for pictures and text aren't included in the subscription. (Exclusions are applicable) But, wait, there's more, on cricut.com, Cricut Access - Paid customers even get free Economy delivery on purchases above $50. This level of membership provides the most accessible and is the better offer overall. This is a yearly-only purchase for just under $120.

You should sign up for Cricut Membership here if you are prepared to delve into infinite amounts of awesome templates and designs. Just sign up with your ID for Cricut.

3.5 Cricut Cartridges

Cricut cartridges are collections of photos and fonts that, like Thanksgiving, the seaside, or springtime, are linked by a theme. Each picture collection may include hundreds of images, styles, or projects and ends up costing between five to thirty bucks.

The cartridges were plastic for the early Cricut machines: physical storage units that you required to insert into the cutting machine to use. You can now link these cartridges or picture sets to your Cricut ID and access them through Cricut Design Space (Explore series) or Cricut Craft Room online (Expression series). You can also buy automated cartridges without caring about trying to interact with those plastic cartridges, getting access to collections of photos digitally.

For the different Cricut Explore models or the Cricut Maker, Praise Cricut, cartridges are no longer needed. The initial Cricut cutter as well as the Cricut Expression series have been developed to be used as standalone devices with actual data cartridges, which do not need a laptop or internet access. With the free Cricut Craft Room computer design software, the Expression machines may be included, but you are still restricted to photos purchased via Cricut cartridges.

There are no cartridges necessary for any of the cutter models typically available by Cricut. Well, if you have a Cricut Explore or a Cricut Builder, and you don't ever want to imagine about a cartridge ever, you're free to go on.

All the outdated cartridges can certainly be used for some of the Cricut electronic machines. Legacy (no longer marketed by Cricut) devices, such as the Expression collection, will be using the cartridges as they still do, through manually putting them into the system and utilizing the keyboard extension, or by attaching them to the device to edit the Cricut Craft Room.

Whatever cartridges you have bought from Cricut can still be used by the newer devices, the Cricut Explore collection, and the Cricut Manufacturer. You have to connect them to the Cricut account first, however, so you can connect them online via Cricut Design Space.

How to Use Cricut Cartridges for Explore Air 2?

They must be connected to the Cricut account in order to utilize cartridges with Cricut Explore Air 2 so that you can use them digitally with Design Space.

(Warning: you may only connect a Cricut cartridge to a specific Cricut account. It is Permanent to link a cartridge: you cannot remove it, and you cannot switch it to another account. Before connecting the cartridges, please make sure that you are signed into the correct Cricut account!)

1. Go on to cricut.com/design, then, on a Windows or Mac device, login into Cricut Design Space. The cartridges cannot be connected via phone or tablet applications.

2. Making sure the Cricut Explore is attached to your computer and switched on.

3. In the upper left corner, press the menu button (it seems like a hamburger: three horizontal bars) and choose 'Connect Cartridges,' around halfway down the menu. The specification for 'Link Cartridges' is outlined in Cricut Design Space.

4. From the drop-down screen, pick the Cricut device.

5. Insert the cartridge into the position on the left-hand side of the Explore cutter, just above 'Open' tab, when prompted. The Cricut cartridge on a Cricut Explore is put into the slot.

The green "Link Cartridge" button will light up after Design Space has identified the cartridge. To link to your cartridge, press the icon.

Design Space can verify "Cartridge linked" as the cartridge is connected to your Cricut account. You will either begin to connect the remainder of your cartridges, access your cartridges, or click the X in the upper right corner to exit the cartridge link dialogue and switch to Cricut Design Space.

IN CRICUT DESIGN SPACE, HOW CAN YOU FIND YOUR CARTRIDGES?

Access to your attached cartridges & purchased photos in the Cricut Design Space is simple.

1. Click the 'Pictures' button on the left-hand menu bar in the open canvas in Design Space to open the Images screen.

2. You'll see three clickable terms around the top: Image Type Cartridges. Select 'Cartridges' to see a chart of all usable Cricut cartridges.

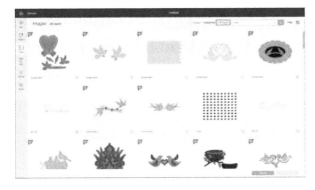

3. In Cricut Design Space, in the top right corner, "Cartridges" being selected. If you just choose to display the cartridges that you currently possess, click on the "Filter" button at the top right of the Photos window and choose "My cartridges." This would contain all cartridges that are free and bought.

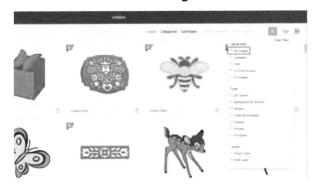

4. In Cricut Design Space, a filtering option is chosen for the cartridges. If you have bought or posted individual photos, remember to check out the Pictures tab as well.

WHAT'S THE CONTRAST BETWEEN CARTRIDGES THAT ARE PHYSICAL & DIGITAL?

Physical cartridges include theme collections of photographs that are loaded onto the cutting machine physically. You will actually use physical cartridges for the Cricut Expression by loading them into the computer and picking and editing the pictures using the keyboard. This physical cartridge may also be connected to your Cricut account utilizing Design Space or Craft Room. When related, the online editing software allows you to quickly view digital copies of the cartridges. You can also hold the physical cartridge, however, or at least snap a pair of front and back images. If you ever have difficulty accessing and need to resync your connected cartridges, Cricut help can ask for these images as evidence that you own the cartridges.

Digital cartridges are thematic collections of pictures purchased digitally and are accessible through Cricut Design Space immediately. They don't have a physical aspect because nothing is going to be sent to you, and you don't need to plug it into the Cricut cutter. While you're linked to the internet and logging into Cricut Design Space, you can use them for all the new Cricut machines.

The Pros

For an inexperienced crafter, cartridges are a fantasy. It can be awesome to make your original designs from scratch, but often it's a little daunting to look at a blank canvas & wonder where to start. You can quickly find motivation with cartridges at hand, divided by every holiday or theme you can think up. Without wasting ages fussing about the template, cartridges are a simple and convenient way to plunge into making DIY vinyl decals & greeting cards.

You can find lots of step-by-step instructions for creating cartridge projects. When you're first practicing how to use a Cricut, these are awesome to use. When you start off, there are too many different topics to learn. Guides make it easier by cutting out all the conjecture. The photographs are deliberately chosen and well-curated in each cartridge. Many creative designers have spent lots of time and money only for you to use in making cartridges! You should be assured that the photos and fonts would be of good quality and function with your Cricut smoothly.

The Cricut Cartridge Collection includes nearly 600 cartridges! There are numerous photographs and projects in each cartridge that can be modified and mixed with various artistic characteristics, offering an exceptional variety of designs. You will still find something which looks perfect with any project you make. There are just too many shapes, designs, and fonts to pick from.

In fact, cartridges are of great importance. You may create hundreds of numerous designs from the core images from only a single cartridge. If you feel that your stock of Cricut cartridges has become too expensive, spend more time playing with the cartridges that you already have, and make use of that innovative value.

It would be great to have a tangible set of Cricut cartridges to find motivation for your next project. You should keep off the internet and search through a large library with your cartridge set instead of trying to gaze through pictures on a screen to locate anything to create.

The Cons

The biggest downside of the cartridge system before the Cricut Explore collection was that you were restricted to what appeared on the cartridges. With the newest Cricut devices, as cartridges are now fully optional, this is no more a drawback! You can still share your own drawings or use SVGs that you find online for free.

One big problem is that you can only connect cartridges to a single account with Cricut. If you are received cartridges or purchase some from e-bay or a thrift store, they can already be connected to someone else's account! It is indefinite to connect cartridges, and you can't switch whose account they are connected to. So, make sure you don't get fooled into getting cartridges that your computer can't really use.

You may feel like you are trapped into the Cricut brand, or perhaps even with a specific machine, after purchasing a bunch of cartridges. For Cricut, this is good, but not so nice for exchanging with the crafting and DIY groups. You can't freely swap your ideas with other individuals if you work with cartridges, one of my favorite aspects of designing new ventures! They can be conveniently exchanged with others and incorporated into the design software for other cutter products, such as Silhouette Workshop, if you use regular old 'SVG files instead.

For each Cricut unit, cartridges don't function the same. You can use cartridges even without internet in the Expressions. For the Cricut Explore Air 2, the cartridge must be connected to your account. And there isn't even a cartridge space in the Cricut Maker! If you want to use photos with a Maker from all your existing cartridges, you'll have to buy Cricut's specific Cartridge Adapter to connect them.

Chapter 4: Cricut Tools and Accessories

4.1 Cricut Accessories You Must Have

1. CRICUT TOOLS (SPECIFICALLY WEEDING TOOL & SCRAPER TOOL)

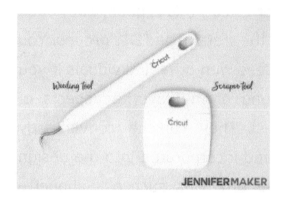

Some simple tools, particularly a weeding accessory & a scraper, are very helpful. You're almost definitely going to want to have a weeding apparatus if you cut Vinyl to extract all the pieces of the Vinyl you don't want to shift to the venture/project. Besides, a scraper is really handy while cutting the paper, as it involves a little while to pick all the tiny jiffs of paper from your mat. You can just get the weeding tool used by Cricut and the scraper apparatus used by Cricut on amazon, so having a Cricut Simple Tool Package on Amazon is a great offer. You'll even notice these devices stocked in the largest craft shops.

Weeding tool

If you want to get a single, most important tool, it's a weeding tool. The weeding tool is utterly necessary for lifting Vinyl, although the spatula and tweezers are good. There are very few different instruments that people use for weeding, and all of them work to remove Vinyl from the backing sheet.

Some other common weeding tools used are:

Pin Pen- On the smallest bits, this tool works great and will pop the vinyl bubbles without tearing as well. While it is comfortable and smooth, it does not twist when peeling to help keep down the Vinyl.

Dental Picks-Users who use dental picks stand by them for weeding. They are great, but maybe the handles are not as convenient.

Exacto knife-To gets into the subtle details; the sharp point is small and reliable enough. To be extra cautious not to damage the project, pair this with tweezers.

2. CRICUT INTEND DEEP-CUT BLADE OR CRICUT KNIFE BLADE (MAKER & EXPLORE)

You should cut thicker materials with the Profound Blade (Explore as well as Maker) and the Knife Blade (just for Maker). If you bought a specific bundle, including it, none of these would come with your Cricut.

If you really want thicker materials to be cut, depending on the machine, you would require either or one or both of the blades.

3. CRICUT SCORING STYLUS/SCORING TOOL

To get acquainted with Cricut accessories, the scoring stylus & scoring kit are all you want. In reality, one of the best things a new Cricut owner needs a scoring system (for Cricut Explore machine) or a scoring accessory (for Cricut Maker owners).

Notice that owners of Cricut Maker can also use the scoring stylus if they wish, but you will receive a better score from the scoring tool. With the help of a scoring gadget, you may create a greater range of paper crafts. It is a simple paper crafting product that creates a huge contrast. Remember that if you're not trying to do paper crafting, you do not require this accessory.

4. Ball of Aluminum FOIL

An aluminum foil ball is all you need to get started with Cricut accessories. A piece of standard aluminum foil for the household firmly balled up.

An aluminum foil ball will help maintain the sharp-point blades smooth and tidy and will hopefully ensure that you don't have to purchase new blades for a long, elongated time. There will be any in your nearest grocery shop, or you can order aluminum foil from Amazon.

5. Adapter for Bluetooth

The older machines from Cricut Explore did not come with Bluetooth activated. You should, however, buy a wireless Bluetooth adapter to connect in and wirelessly use your phone.

6. Kits of Tools

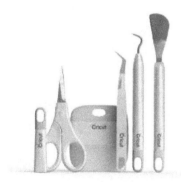

Purchasing one of the toolkits is the most affordable way to obtain the tools you would need most frequently. With tweezers, weeders, scissors, spatula, and scraper, the simple toolset comes along. This is perfect if you're mainly going to do designs of Vinyl or iron-on. All in the standard toolkit plus scoring stylus, paper trimmer, and new blade for the trimmer come with the necessary tool kit. For paper crafters, this is the dream kit.

7. The spatula

The tool you definitely should have is the spatula. You don't want to think about ripping the cloth while you're moving material off the cutting mat. The spatula takes control of this by the quick and simple removal of material from the mat. To maintain the mat clean and clutter-free, the spatula could also be used with the scraper.

8. The Tweezers

They are super handy if you don't have tweezers, though. The tweezers for weeding are the Needle Point Tweezers from Pazzles. Such tweezers have a sharp edge, which makes Vinyl outstanding. Without trying to use the edges, certain points are intense enough to grab Vinyl right from the center. Even they will pick up the smallest tiny scrap!

The other tweezes are specifically built to pick up and keep objects in place. The Cricut Tweezers are no more marketed individually but are sold in the Essential Tool Package only. If you're still looking for a decent pair, the Craft Tweezers EK tools are efficient! They are perfect for using reverse activity to pick up rhinestones as well as other adornments. It's a perfect reversal action because you don't get sore palms.

9. Scissors

A world of improvement can be created with the proper scissors for the task. The Cricut Scissors are crafted with blades of polished stainless steel, making even cuts while staying robust.

The scissors are very sharp and equipped with a mico-tip blade, so it's quicker and easier to focus on the intricate points in smaller areas right down to the point. It also has an adjustable, secure, colored end cap, which makes it easier to comfortably store the scissors. In a variety pack that contains 8'' fabric scissors and 5'' art scissors, Cricut offers the scissors.

The Cutter Bee Accurate Scissors are an awesome replacement to the Cricut brand scissors. For years, they've been my mom's and my go-to craft scissors, and they're still really sharp.

You'll want to get a specific pair of fabric scissors if you intend to undertake several fabric projects. With drab scissors, nothing is harder than having to cut cloth, but nothing amplifies scissors quicker than paper.

10. Cutters/Trimmers for Paper

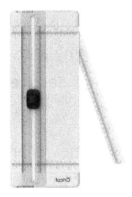

When you try to get direct cuts, a paper cutter is only super convenient. Do not use a ruler and scissors anymore. A paper trimmer, particularly while you

Are dealing with Vinyl, makes cutting so much simpler. Cricut has a trimmer of its own, but the Fiskars Sure Cut Paper Trimmer is a little more advanced. To get the ideal folds, it also has the choice of scoring.

11. Brayer

You'll want to buy yourself a brayer whether you're dealing with a cloth or bigger Vinyl (or something, really). One of the most popular mistakes that beginners make is not thoroughly stabilizing material before cutting, to learn what other top mistakes are in my post. By letting the material adhere to the Cricut mat despite harming it, a brayer solves this.

Using firm, even pressure, you run straight the roller over the material on the cutting mat to get it to hold properly and eliminate any wrinkles. It may also be used in a number of other applications, such as vinyl or ink-blocking applications.

12. Additional Mats

Something that you can have a backup or are mats as well. When you are in the midst of the task and know the mats are no stickier, there's nothing more irritating. There are places to stick the cutting mats that could save money but keeping extra mats on hand is always a smart idea.

For the kinds of mats, you use more often, you'll want extra mats. Make sure that you get mats with the correct material:

LightGrip (Blue) - for projects on paper and cardstock

StandardGrip (Green) - for iron and Vinyl

StorngGrip (Purple) - For poster board, dense cardstock as well as other heavier fabrics,

FabricGrip (Pink) - For fabric

BrightPad

For a number of factors, the BrightPad is superb. First, by having the cut lines clear, it allows weeding so much simpler. If you have more than a quick cut, lots of that can work out. For tracking and modifying designs, you may also use it.

4.2 Cricut Supplies

CARDSTOCK

You'll need cardstock while the need to start doing paper craft items with the Cricut precise towards the way. Paper-filled 12x12 scrapbook paper storage organizer

VINYL

You'll need Vinyl whether you want to begin and producing vinyl projects instantly with the Cricut. For a number of vinyl designs. If you want to produce posters, car window stickers, coffee mugs and bottles, these are the things you'll want.

Permanent Vinyl-great even over wears and tear for designs you want to continue.

Adjustable Vinyl-good for projects that you don't want to last forever. Excellent for rentals and much more!

Glitter Vinyl-Removable Sparkle Vinyl

Dry Erase Vinyl-ideal for tagging

Chalkboard Vinyl-great for calendar creation or even for marking

If you choose to make handmade signs or screen printed shirts, use this Stencil Vinyl.

Holographic Vinyl-same as standard Vinyl, except with varying colors based on the position you are looking at

Printable vinyl-great for sticker creation

Patterned Vinyl apply some interesting themes to your projects, from Mickey & Minnie to Star Wars, watercolor and adorable hippos.

Such Material Packs are perfect if you're trying to get a selection of pieces! They come with a range of tools for cutting, tools and some even come with a Cricut cutie.

ADHESIVE FOIL has a pleasing shine to it, comparable to Vinyl. It can be tougher to weed/apply. If you're new to dealing with Vinyl, before you start using foil, use plain Vinyl.

IRON-ON-This is what you're going to use for shirts, cushions, caps, etc.

Everyday Iron-On, perfect for about every project to use! The most compact and accessible in several colors and packs

Bring sparkle to every project with **Glitter Iron-On**. Very quick to weed and to add

Holographic Iron-On: Add dimension either with opal holographic or holographic glitter to your designs

Foil Iron-On-To your designs, add shine.

Patterned Iron-On, apply those interesting designs to your projects, from Mickey and Minnie to Star Wars, watercolor and adorable hippos.

Stretchy iron-on, perfect to use on athletic apparel, Sport Flex Iron-On

Making every shirt look like a sweater, **Mesh Iron-On**,

Iron-On Prototypes-pre-made designs that can be used alone or tailored to some kind of iron-on style.

INFUSIBLE INK

NEWEST product from Cricut. To infuse ink onto clothes, tote bags and more, Infusible Ink involves heating from an Easy Press and Heat Press to send you a professionally designed project with results forever! Read more online on how it operates.

- Infusible Sheets for Ink Transfer

- Infusible Pens and Markers with Ink

- Blanks of Infusible Ink

Good for creating invitations, gift bags, gift boxes, and scrapbooking.

CARDSTOCK

Good for creating jewelry, key chains, hair bows, and infant moccasins.

FAUX LEATHER.

GENUINE LEATHER-great for creating a home furniture, shoes, and more.

FELT is best for designing finger marionettes, adornments, masks and bandanas.

WINDOW CLING is great for walls, refrigerators and other equipment for temporary tasks.

FABRIC-FOR CRICUT MAKER ONLY-fabric bundles that are suitable for every sewing project.

14. THE TAPE USED FOR TRNSFEREING-TRANSFER TAPE

The Vinyl design projects will require a minimum of one transfer tape roll to enable you to transfer the Vinyl to the surface of the project. Be guaranteed to get the Standard Grip Tape for Cricut, not the transfer tape of Strong Grip (that is just used for shimmery Vinyl).

15. EXTRA CRICUT MATS

In order to function properly, certain designs may really require a fresh or relatively new mat, which is quite soggy. You should wash them; it is preferred that you partake a minimum of one of the mats used by Cricut, and if you want to undertake some bigger projects, maybe any of the 12" x 24" mats. Cricut has a range of mat packs that include 12 "x12" Light, Basic and Firm Grip mats. In 12" x24" or in multi-packs, you can even get them extra-long. Just be sure you have the correct mat for the device and supplies. In contrast to Explore and Maker, the Cricut Joy uses unique mats.

16. CRICUT EASY PRESS

The Easy Press is a perfect accessory if you're trying to do iron-on vinyl designs, which makes things easier.

17. PENS USED FOR CRICUT

Pick up a couple of Cricut pens while you ponder, you're going to try to do some envelope wrapping or inscription in common. The apt accurate in the accessory clasp. They even work on tags and designs of cards for writing.

What you need to get started with Cricut accessories are Cricut pens!

Cloth and fabric labeling pen

You'll notice it cuts fabric very well if there's a Cricut Maker. So, a limited stock of felt as well as other fabrics might be handy! You would also dearth to buy the pen for fabric marking.

And if you might be tempted, you don't need any color and form of cardstock and Vinyl.

18. Cricut Access

A trial version of Cricut Access is a catalog of photos, ventures, and fonts that comes with your latest Cricut cutting machine. It's all within the software Cricut Design Studio (the software you used or are going to use to configure your Cricut). Thus, it's advised that you select Ventures, pick 'Cricut Access subscription' from the top drop-down menu and choose a task that guises like what you want. Certain ventures will be tougher to do.

Every card is a double-sheeted project, but you'll have to freight additional mat into the machine with some other piece of cardstock. Design Space can display to you which color is going to be cut subsequent, or you may choose any colors you choose.

You may find several free SVG archives, or you might purchase them, too. Many of the archives (SVG) in the resource library are free to copy and to be used.

Chapter 5: DIY Cricut Projects

5.1 How to Start Your First Project?

Cricut offers a whole new universe of compossibilities, whether you're trying to take the paper crafts to the next juncture or make personalized clothes and décor. Cut, compose and score your creative creations with the Cricut Explore and Maker machines on a massive variety of materials: cardstock, fabric, iron-on vinyl, wood, plastic, tracing paper & more.

We are natural artists with imaginations who can create incredible and extraordinary possessions. The device can support the development of these excellent crafts. A Cricut is a smooth cutting machine used in the manufacturing of crafts. Simple Paper, Washi Sheets, card stock, vinyl, faux leather, plastic & more would be cut. Yeah, the stuff you can do with a machine from Cricut.

What do you intend for the Cricut machine to start operating?

Design Space Program is used by Cricut machines and is very simple to understand. To run the program, you would require an Android or Apple- device, tablet, or smartphone.

5.2 Which Is The Right Cricut For Beginners?

The Cricut machine (Explore Air 2) is the perfect cutting machine for novices, advanced and skilled crafters, according to user reports. It proposes covenant software learning, fresh cutting, and excellent group support and suggestions focused on projects.

For the novice, Cricut enables crafting quite enough easier. Think about each minute that you save from doing the whole cutting and drafting for you handled by a machine. Beginner Cricut crafts and intermediate Cricut crafts are approved, yet all crafts and inventions created with the Cricut machine are sure to be magnificent. It might seem complicated the 1st time you attempt anything, but these simple Cricut ventures for newcomers are fantastic.

It's nice to be willing to give someone a handmade present. This is rendered super simple by the Cricut machine, and the choices as a novice are endless. Following are a couple of perfect novices Cricut ventures great for presents.

1. FLOWER CORSAGE

You will need the mentioned supplies to make a flower

Things you need

- Cardstock (in your color choice for flowers and leaves) (in your color choice for flowers and leaves)

- The Glue

- SCISSORS

- Pins or ribbons

- Template for Free

Directions

1. Print the template on your card stock color choice and cut the flower template. To quickly cut these, we use Cricut Explore.

2. Spray the paper gently with water (this will make it much easier to fold the paper into the forms you want) and curve the paper to form shapes.

3. On each flower segment and leaves, glue the tabs together and allow them to dry.

4. Using watercolors or markers, apply bright edges (optional). Weld together all the petals and leaves to create a flower and let it dry.

5. If you make a wrist corsage, cut the appropriate length of the ribbon, bind to the ribbon with the finished flower

6. Put one on the rear of the flower for gift-giving if you are using pins. Cover a cellophane bag or a keepsake box with the completed corsage.

This flower corsage is a simple, economical way to offer your mom a lovely, handmade present. Surprise her and make her day with this imaginative present.

2. DOLLAR STORE BURLAP FALL WREATHS

Things you need

- Straw Wreath, Noodle Pool or Wreath Foam

- Ribbon Burlap

- Free Printable or Your own or Cricut Embellishments

- Sewing Pins of Glass Head

Directions

1. Grab materials.

2. Wrap the burlap cloth across the straw wreath.

3. For the straw wreath, tie the edges of the ribbon.

4. Cut the available pintables by hand and use a Cricut and make a link

5. To tie flowers or bats and the moon to the wreath, utilize push pins.

6. Add ribbons and hang them anywhere in your house.

3. DIY COFFEE MUG

Things you need

- Cricut Explore/Machine for silhouette cutting

- 12 x 12 Cutting Mat for Cricut

- SVG file

- The Permanent Vinyl

- Tape for transferring

- Mugs for Coffee

Directions

1. Gather supplies for more details

2. Use your Cricut or Model cutting machine to cut the SVG picture (or your own image), then weed the picture.

3. Attach the transfer tape to the weeded picture, peel the vinyl paperback, and pull firmly on the mug with the image.

4. Peel the transfer tape back, and you're done!

Now you learned how to create a personalized mug with Cricut and how to use a Cricut machine to make a coffee mug.

4. DIY PIECE OF MY HEART PUZZLE CARD

Things you need

- Explore Cricut Machine Cutting

- The software of Cricut Design Space

- Jen Goode-designed Puzzle & Card

- Standard Grip Cricut® mat 12'' x 12''

- Cardstock in White and Red

- Glue

Directions

1. Print and cut the heart pattern, following the directions on the screen.

2. Assemble the puzzle and draw on the back of your own private message. By using the soft stick mat, you will briefly keep the puzzle together (the blue one).

3. Organize the envelope and inside put the components of the puzzle.

5. DIY MINI CHRISTMAS BOX AND BOW

- Cricut Machine & Cricut Design Space

- Cardstock in different colors

- ADHESIVE

Directions

1. Upload the SVG cut file gift box to Cricut Design Space.

2. Measure to the dimensions of preference.

3. Fold and glue to the end of the main body flap, and then fold it into the tabs.

4. Fill it with something you'd like.

5. Tabs to Fold Top. If you'd like, glue them together.

6. Attach a bow and ribbon.

7. Glue together the edges of each bow loop to attach the bow. To make each layer of loops for the bow, glue the centers respectively. Add a second layer of loops for it. Glue the bow's back, and then wrap it in position with the tiny centerpiece and glue.

6. DIY HELLO SUMMER KITCHEN TOWEL

Things you need

- Machine for cutting Cricut Maker

- Account for Cricut Design Space

- Jen Goode's Triple Scoop Cake Cone Cut Template

- Fine Tip Blade

- Easy Press 2

- Access to Cricut Design Space

- Three shades for the scoops & one for the cone, Iron on Kitchen Towel for Kitchens

Directions

1. Open the Space Cut File for Arrangement and scale it to match the kitchen towel.

2. Ungroup the pic.

3. Highlight each part and pick the file to cut. The drawing portion of this cut file has to be deleted.

4. Add the text above the ice cream cone and below it.

5. Curve the text above the cone using the curve function.

6. Give a cut to the project. On a standard grip cutting mat, put the iron on it. Until you cut, don't forget to mirror the pic.

7. Weed the surplus iron-on and repeat with each color.

8. Pre-Heat Easy Press 2 as per the heat settings suggested by Cricut.

9. On the towel, put the ice cream cone and press it in place. Layer the scoops of ice cream on top of the cone one at a time. Then, just include the text.

7. DIY MAGNETIC CHORE CHART

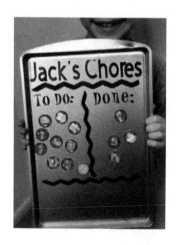

Things you need

- Cookie sheet

- Flat-edge translucent glass marbles, 1''

- You will need some sort of transparent adhesive if you are using marbles.

- Epoxy Magnet Paper (just make sure that it would be small enough for your machine to cut.

- Printable Paper for Sticker

- Blade with the Deep Cut

- Adhesive Vinyl or Adhesive Foil of the chosen color

- Transferring Tape

- A project of Design Space for Magnets and Vinyl

Directions

1. Open and configure the Design Space Project. You should modify the name, font used, etc., in this file until we get underway (or add different chores).

2. Follow these guidelines on how to use Cricut to create magnets. You can miss the section about making them and go to step four right away.

3. You will then cut out the remainder of the project with vinyl or sticky foil using your fine point blade until you cut out the magnets.

4. Once the components are cut out, the residual material is weeded out.

5. And transfer the stuff to your cookie tray using transfer tape.

6. And now, you're done.

5.3 Tips and Tricks for Cricut Projects

It can be super daunting to start off as a novice user of Cricut. You have no idea what to do, what you need to know, and where to get started. These Cricut tips are some excellent hacks from professional crafters that would save you significant money and stress as you don't have an infinite budget or time. Check out the ones

1. Prior to your first use, prepare the Standard Grip mats.

In reality, if you placed paper right on that mat, you can end up ripping the paper when you attempt to eliminate it. These green mats can be quite sticky. Your mat seasoning could make a huge difference.

Why are you seasoning a cutting mat for Cricut? Simply put on the mat a sheet of plain paper, clean it down, and carry it up. Repeat a couple of times to make sure you are making your way around the whole mat. This will help minimize the mat's initial "bite," which can be very harsh and destroy your materials, particularly the paper projects!

2. To make it wear uniformly, move your mat.

With the silhouette arrow (also the dangling position) pointing toward the machine, most Cricut users load the mats. But, with time, the plastic can wear down and allow it to crack, and it has to be changed.

- **How to make it last longer with the Cricut mat?**

Rotate it in order to prolong the life of the mat. Try to alternate aiming the tiny silhouette arrow often to the machine AND other times to yourself. Anyway, the mat may load, and this will actually increase the Cricut mat lifetime. Just try to ensure that the supplies are still mounted in the upper left corner on whichever hand you have pointed to your machine.

3. How to use a broken or damaged Cricut mat?

Does it have a break in your mat, so you just need to have one more cut out of it? With these mats, cracks, cuts, and normal wear and tear or just realities of life, this is, after all, a cutting machine. And what if the mat isn't yet ready for you to get out of? Or what if you only need yet another cut out of it.

Mark a piece of tape on the rear of the mat. Trying to cover the damaged section entirely. This, at least briefly, will help stabilize it, so you can begin the idea.

4. How to install a bounding box to promote weeding projects?

Attach a bounding box to the IN Design Space Studio. Whatever fits better for your design, cover your design with a box or circle in the Canvas process.

This would carve an outline around the design such that the negative stuff is simpler to weed away from the design.

5. Do you have a lot of little, complicated information to weed out of your project?

A substitute for the weeding of minor information from the project. To collect all those little bits, try running a gunk roller over the project.

Might not get most of them, and it might get more than you expect, particularly on very complicated projects, sparing you a bunch of time and energy.

6. Stop stressing and worrying, if the setting you have selected is right, if the stress is appropriate, etc.

Only turn it over to Custom. It's a set-and-forget plan that works beautifully.

This helps you to directly pick the settings in Design Space and adjust them from there.

7. Want to dip the toes into the making of stencils without losing precious resources such as vinyl or acetate?

With your Cricut, you may cut stencils out of freezer paper. This is a perfect, inexpensive stencil choice and is something that you probably have in the kitchen already.

Best of all, you have many more if anything goes bad, because compared to other materials such as vinyl and acetate, it costs pennies.

8. Using Glad Press 'n Seal as a really cheap replacement rather than transferring paper

This is a terrific hack in a mess. Using contact paper, which works well for moving photos for around $5 on Amazon and at Walmart, is a perfect budget-friendly alternative that works even more.

9. Remove small pieces with a gooey lint roller from the Cricut cutouts.

A lint roller may also be used to clear glitter from the cutting mat and tends to hold them sticky at the very same time! Sincerely, this is like a hack from 3-for-1.

10. Cheap way for the Cricut Mat to clean up

The best method of washing mats efficiently and conveniently is just basic Daily cleaner and hot water. Or, choose a non-alcoholic baby wipe if it's only a short cleanup. Some persons, however, stand by Awesome spray (yep, that's the brand name) that you can purchase at the Dollar Store.

11. How to get the mat sticky again?

It will look SUPER sticky when you first use your mat. It will start losing the stickiness over time, however, but this is a perfect trick to make it last longer so that you don't have to fix them so much (saving money again!)

Simply tape your mat using painter's tape off the sides and gently spray this fantastic stuff on your mat to bring the sticky back.

Recent mats are really too sticky. Before the first task, you might also want to rub your hands all across them several times to help "wear" them in. Always make sure that the correct mat is used. Initially, the green mat would be too messy for the cardstock, so you'll want to choose the blue mat.

12. Using a credit card / older gift card to rub the layout well for an easy transfer following weeding if you lose your burnishing method.

13. To produce a stencil that is basically free, cut freezer paper with your Cricut. A nice trick if, for instance, you want to create a wooden sign.

14. To avoid pet hairs or dust from clinging to them, hold the plastic sheet that corresponds with your mats and place it back on after usage.

15. To quickly extract scraps while weeding, wrap covering up or painting tape across your palm.

16. Label the top of your mat to prevent errors:

To make sure you load it right, label the upper part of your cutting mat. This is essential for beginners to prevent costly faults that could involve cutting thru your mat if improperly loaded!

17. with the latest fonts, spice up the layouts.

At dafont.com, find a Lot of free options. If you use them on items you sell, you may require a certificate for professional use. Just be cautious.

5.4 How to Sell Your Cricut Products

Few Tips for making money With Cricut.

1. Intended to be unique

In general, just be yourself. Bring to the table your strangeness and innovation. In the designing universe, that's how it works, isn't it? But you may be one of the first individuals to get on a wave trend ride before the next popular seller comes along. But if you're not patient, the process of selling Cricut crafts may get tiresome and expensive.

Upgrade your crafts at Cricut and put your own emphasis on increasing profit margin trends. Don't be frightened of changing fonts even. Super promotions and freebies for quality fonts can be found at fontbundles.net, something that easy would help you look professional with fonts.

And when the craft appears like someone else's, the fact is, it's only going to become a trade battle. Nobody's expecting to win.

2. Keeping it refined

You will think that producing and selling something under the sun would give you more diversity, thus more clients, hence more income. That's not the way it goes, however.

More prices, more exhaustion, and more non-selling goods are what it would bring you.

Do not aspire to be the design world's Walmart; aim to be a professional, and the best of your field of craftiness is there. So, take a moment to determine what you are going to be remembered for.

3. be impervious

Work regularly on the Cricut craft venture. Preferably, each day you can be focusing on it. Any of you might only choose to offer it as a passion and might only be willing to work once a week on it.

Do so as frequently as you can, whatever the routine is. If you neglect your businesses for days or months, or years, you're never able to get far.

Be compliant with prices and also with consistency. Your clients need to know what to demand from you. If they feel they can rely on you, they can suggest you to everyone else over and over.

4. Tenacious wins

There are bound to be days where clients piss you off. There'll be days where nothing works smoothly. You're going to bust your butt and easily going nowhere. Be courageous when you make your Cricut money; never relinquish.

5. How much do you want?

Please go through all of your materials and measure up the costs for the love of all things crafty. You'll be well able to price the goods for sale until you have the expense of materials. If you enjoy working for free, don't overlook the time it would take you to create the products.

A basic rule of thumb is that the purchase price would be between two and four times your supply cost. Don't fear because people are snickering at you that it's too much. You're the original, you've narrowed the scope down, and you're a professional, and you're the best at what you're doing. Plus, you use premium merchandise (more on that soon). People would pay for it happily.

6. Learn something new every day

Do not be ashamed of knowing about others before you have left. You don't have to find out all by yourself.

Everyone else has already accomplished it if you want to understand how to ascend the Etsy rankings or build a good Facebook community, and now they teach all the tips and techniques they know.

At least you'll be doing more advertising than crafting at the start of the Cricut Company. Making it a priority to discover something fresh that applies to your business every day.

7. Control of quality

Selling standard products. Any day of the week, quality dominates over quantities.

People are going to pay for quality, and for quality, they will suggest you to their mates. The most that you can do is the word of mouth marketing.

Conclusion

The Cricut machine is a very successful creation. It has enabled scrapbookers and many others with their desires, not only limited to the field of scrapbook making, but also to other aspects. There are several advantages of owning one of these machines, and Cricut has taken everyone by storm. The Explore and the Maker are so extremely versatile that one of these machines actually derives from a number of ventures people use with blogs or social networking.

As many people would realize and are conscious of, while crafters do a number of work that never see the light of day, they do just as many as they do, and you can still go back to certain projects later and expand them before finishing them with the saving option that this machine gives you. If a holiday has arrived and you do not have a present, or if there are last-minute activities coming up and you will need cool ideas to carry them with you, this may be a perfect choice for you.

Style is still a key concern in the scrapbook. Choosing a template in the past could cause migraines of monumental dimensions, but that is a different matter now. The Cricut machine itself is only liable for cutting papers on the basis of a particular pattern or design,

Vinyl, and fabric. You may create or modify the pattern or layout via a software program called the Cricut Design Space. Go for Cricut cartridges if you are searching for simple and well-defined designs that have already been built-in. For the templates that are already in effect, there is no limit on what you may make. The basic rule is to let your creativity run wild. This is a product that any potential scrap-booker wants to have. Besides being a cutter with designs for a scrapbook, the Cricut machine has many applications.

CPSIA information can be obtained
at www.ICGtesting.com
Printed in the USA
LVHW011705220221
679517LV00004B/168